The
ULTIMATE
PRAYER
BOOK

7 Minutes
to Change Your Day . . .
Your Life . . . and Your World . . .

Fred Williams

WESTBOW
PRESS®
A DIVISION OF THOMAS NELSON
& ZONDERVAN

WestBow Press books may be ordered through booksellers or by contacting:

WestBow Press
A Division of Thomas Nelson & Zondervan
1663 Liberty Drive
Bloomington, IN 47403
www.westbowpress.com
1 (866) 928-1240

ISBN: 978-1-9736-1773-0 (sc)
ISBN: 978-1-9736-1772-3 (e)

Print information available on the last page.

WestBow Press rev. date: 05/09/2018

ACKNOWLEDGEMENTS

When you've been on this earth 50 plus years as I have, you think back often about the people you've interacted with; people you've met and people with whom you've shared your life. The people who God has allowed you to cross paths with have in some ways made your life what it is. I want to acknowledge some of those people in my life who have had the biggest influence on me. I have to start at the top with God, Jesus Christ and the Holy Spirit. I was drawn into relationship with Him in my early 20s and can never thank Him enough for giving me "Life" and for the blessings and provision He has given me. Initially He used a man named Clark to speak to me. Clark walked the walk before he talked the talk, and I saw it in him. I was led to Calvary Chapel a few years later where "Pastor Bob," was used more than anyone in my life to teach me about the bible and the Christian life. He brought in a worship leader named Clay, who is simply the best, and taught me to worship by taking not-so-fun "church" music and bringing it alive and into a way of life.

I want to thank my parents, without whom I wouldn't be here - they have ALWAYS, ALWAYS supported me in every possible way imaginable. My wife, my soul mate, who of the humans I know is the best example of Christianity. Without her support and love, I wouldn't be me. My children, who are the joy of my life, who understand me and the decisions I've made. My sister, my only sibling; although we are chronologically distant, geographically distant, we are finally getting to where we should always have been. And finally Joe Devlin, who I met over 30 years ago, but God has used in the last few months to pull this together and edit what you're reading today.

Thank you all!

PREFACE

This is a book about prayer. I hope everyone who claims to believe God exists will read it with an open mind. There is great power in prayer, we all need it, we would all like to have it, but few ever find that power. As you read this book you **will** find it and you **will** have the Spirit of God flow through you like through a branch from the vine with the purpose of giving life and bearing fruit. This fruit is the most satisfying fruit you will ever experience on this earth. This life will be the most gratifying you can possibly imagine. This will help you find God's purpose for your life.

There are two foundational biblical verses on which this book is built. In the book of Ephesians, the tenth verse of the second chapter states, *For we are God's workmanship, created in Christ Jesus to do good works, which God prepared in advance for us to do.* My hope for this journey you are about to take is to find those works that God almighty has for you to do and live a truly fulfilling life as a result of doing those works. The second verse is in the book of Philippians, the sixth verse of the first chapter, which states *being confident of this, that He who began a good work in you will carry it on to completion until the day of Christ Jesus.* God will be faithful with His end; we just need to be faithful with ours. God does have a plan for your life; this book will take you there.

Instructional note: If you are not already familiar with the bible, you will see many italicized verses as you read, taken from the bible. They are written as "book, chapter, and verse." For example, John 3:16 signifies the book of John, the third chapter, the 16th verse.

CONTENTS

INTRODUCTION

Do you pray to God? You should. He wants to hear from you **and** He has things to say to you. If you're not praying to Him you'll never find out what those things may be, and believe me, you want to know. Are you willing to listen?

What if there was a prayer that would lead you to a much deeper level of intimacy with God Himself? What if there was an "Ultimate" prayer? What if this prayer took you just 7 minutes, and with that, changed your life dramatically?

I believe such a prayer exists. I think there are many people who could pray this prayer and achieve amazing things in their lives; things they had no idea God could accomplish through them.

Everyone knows, and would probably agree, that prayer is good...but the "Ultimate Prayer?" Well, your "Ultimate Prayer" has the potential to take you to a whole new place in your life. Take this journey, this challenge; and you just may find God's will for your life.

CHAPTER ONE

GETTING RIGHT

Before you even start seeking the "Ultimate" prayer, you have to be right with God. This is not about a particular religion, because **man** made religion. God wants a **relationship** with man. To be right with God, you must have a relationship with Him. This relationship must be on His terms, not yours. All you need to know about having a relationship with Him is found in His book. The book that He inspired is a complete book written about the beginnings of this earth through what will be the end of it. His book, the bible, is a history book; it's a book of prophecy; it's a drama, and it's a love story. It consists of 66 individual books written by over 40 authors from three different continents over a 1500 year period of time in three different languages. The more you read it, the more you'll get to know Him, and you will realize He **is** amazing. You will *want* to have a **relationship** with Him.

In the first chapter of the bible it explains how we were made in His image, **Genesis 1:27,** *So God created man in His own image, in the image of God He created him; male and female He created them* (NIV). He provided a place to live and lots of freedom but warned of just one thing: **Genesis 2:17,** *You are free to eat from any tree in the garden; but you must not eat from the tree of the knowledge of good and evil, for when you eat of it you will surely die* (NIV). We know that Adam and Eve ended up getting tricked into eating from that tree, and that significant decision changed everyone's relationship with God forever. The first three chapters in the book of Genesis tell the story, but the relevance is that they no longer had God (who is a Spirit) living in and through them. They were perfect in being made in His image (they were "spiritually alive"), but after ignoring God's one rule, they died. We know that this death was not a physical death, Adam and Eve went on living for some time, but a spiritual death. God withdrew His Spirit from them, and everyone born since is born in the flesh but not with God's Spirit within them. We have a problem; we need to get right with God…

The next step in history occurred in the days of Moses; God always has a plan. In that day, He gave us commands and laws to live by so we could have a right relationship with Him. God is holy, so for anyone to be right with God, they have to be holy as well. If you wanted to be holy or right with Him, you would just have to abide by all His laws, and there were over 600 of those. God is omniscient or all-knowing, so He knew there was no way for people to do this; in fact, failure was a certainty. He knew that living without Him in us, we would not live by all the laws and therefore we would 'sin.' This is why in the New Testament He states in **Romans 3:20**, *Therefore, no one will be declared righteous in His sight by observing the law; rather through the law we become conscious of sin* (NIV). With this consciousness of sin (the word sin is another way of saying to miss the mark), He needed to give us a way to be covered. This way, we could stay "right" with Him through the covering of our sins.

Those who lived in the days of Moses had the opportunity to have their sins covered. They would take one of their animals to be sacrificed for the covering of their sin. They would take this sacrifice to their temple and the high priest would take it into a holy place, he would sprinkle its blood, and their sins would be covered. It's described in the Old Testament book of **Leviticus 17:11**, *For the life of a creature is in the blood, and I have given it to you to make atonement for yourselves on the altar; it is the blood that makes atonement for one's life* (NIV). In the New Testament it's described in **Hebrews 10:22**, *In fact, the law requires that nearly everything be cleansed with blood, and without the shedding of blood there is no* *forgiveness* (NIV). So there you have it! If you lived then, you would take your sin, and your animal sacrifice for your sin, and it would be taken care of. Okay, but what about now? What about your sins today? The fact is we all sin in one way or another; every day, in most people's cases. We somehow, some way, will miss the mark. The book of Romans confirms this in **Romans 3:23**, *for all have sinned and fall short of the glory of God* (NIV). So what do **we** do about that?

All through the Old Testament there were references to a coming "Messiah." This Messiah would not just cover the sins of mankind but would actually take them away. These references or prophecies can point us to this Messiah and help us all be right with God through Him and His actions. If you read through these prophesies, it will be obvious who this Messiah is. These prophesies include His place of birth, **Micah 5:2** (written about 750 BC), His time of birth, **Daniel 9:25** (written about 600 BC), the fact that He would be born of a virgin, **Isaiah 7:14** (written about 750 BC), how He would "arrive," **Zechariah 9:9** (written about 500 BC) and the fact that He would rise again. There are dozens of prophecies that confirm that Jesus Christ is this Messiah.

Let's step back then, and figure this all the way through. Here we are today, being born without the Spirit of God in us, so we are in fact spiritually dead, and without any covering for our sin. Your spiritually dead parents could not give you something that they did not possess, so you are not born "right" with God; you are essentially separated from Him from the start. Even if you're a "good" person, you still have sinned and missed the mark (and I don't recommend killing an animal and taking it to your priest or pastor). God does want a relationship with you, however, He's holy and you're not, so He **cannot** have a relationship with you under those circumstances. Finally, in a perfect way, He created the way to make us right with Him. The bible states in **2 Corinthians 5:21**, *God made Him who had no sin to be sin for us, so that in Him we might become the righteousness of God* (NIV). God chose a virgin woman to bear this Messiah who, because He was not of human descent, actually **had** the Spirit of God alive in Him. He would not just cover our sins but completely forgive them. This is illustrated in **John 1:29** where He is described as the Lamb of God who **takes away** our sins, not just covers them. When He lived on earth, He lived by the law because in fact He was God, and therefore He was able to live without sin (as you can read throughout the entire New Testament). Then, He gave up His life for us. That Spirit of God is now available for us to receive, making us right! In **John 1:12-13**, *Yet to all who **receive** Him, to those who **believe** in His name, He gave the right to become children of God; children born not of natural descent, nor of human decision or a husband's will, but born of God* (NIV). We have simply to understand this, believe this, and receive it into our hearts and we will be right with God!

You may want to read that last paragraph again; it is the most amazing concept to fathom on this earth and in our lives. The fact that the holy, sovereign God, the maker and creator of this universe desires to have a relationship with us, and through something **He** did, we can have a right relationship with Him. If we receive Him on His terms, we are righteous in His sight; **Psalm 34:17**, *The righteous cry out and the Lord hears them* (NIV). God will hear your prayers based on these facts. We are now in a position to pray to Him based on His Word, and be confident that He hears us! **Ephesians 3:12**, *In Him and through faith in Him we may approach God with freedom and confidence* (NIV).

This concept is simple in some ways, but not always simple to grasp, so let me explain it another way. The bible clearly states in **John 14:6**, *I am the way and the truth and the life, no one comes to the Father except through me* (NIV). Jesus paid the ultimate price, and if you reject that gift, you can't be right with God, period. I didn't say it, I'm just reiterating it. **1 John 2:23**, *No one who denies the Son has the Father; whoever acknowledges the Son has the Father* (NIV). Once again it seems quite clear, don't let religion complicate it. Simply put, there is a time in every person's life when this decision must be made. This decision is a "rebirth" event. It's stated clearly in the book of **John 3:1-7,** *Now there was a man of the Pharisees named Nicodemus, a member of the Jewish ruling counsel. He came to Jesus at night end and said, "Rabbi, we know you are a teacher who has come from God. For no one could perform the miraculous signs you are doing if God were not with him." In reply Jesus said, "I tell you the truth, no one can see the Kingdom of God unless he is born again." "How can a man be born when he is old?" Nicodemus asked. "Surely he cannot enter a second time into his mother's womb to be born!" Jesus answered, "I tell you the truth, no one can enter the Kingdom of God unless he is born of water and the Spirit. Flesh gives birth to flesh, but Spirit gives birth to spirit." You should not be surprised at my saying "You must be born again"* (NIV). I know this term "born again" scares people, they immediately think of religious extremes and fanaticism. Maybe we should call it a **spiritual rebirth** for that's what it really is, a spiritually dead person now gaining a spiritual life. The fact is, without this, you cannot be right with God and the "Ultimate" prayer cannot be a reality for you. Prayer has tremendous potential, but not coming from an unrighteous person. Get right with God by starting a relationship with Him. **James 5:16,** *The prayer of a righteous man is powerful and effective* (NIV).

If you know that you've already experienced this, if you know for a fact that you have a right relationship with God through Jesus Christ, excellent! If you are uncertain as to whether you have achieved it, Chapter 2 will show you how to get right, and how to move forward in your Ultimate Prayer!

CHAPTER TWO

SALVATION CONFIRMATION

This chapter is written specifically for a person who is unsure about whether or not they will go to heaven when they die. One thing is for certain, 100% of humans will die. If you looked at humans across the globe, the average lifespan is about 67 years. In the United States it's about 79 years. Japan boasts the highest lifespan at about 83, and Swaziland (Near South Africa) has one of the lowest at around 49 years (2015, World Health Organization Data, retrieved from https://en.wikipedia.org/wiki/Life_expectancy).

Most people who are asked this question: "Do you believe in God?" - would most likely answer "of course, who doesn't?" Sadly there are some who do not even believe God exists, but let's for the sake of this discussion address the high percentage of people who do believe in the existence of God. According to data from the Pew Research Center, approximately 70% of Americans are considered Christian, the most popular segments being approximately 50% Protestant (various denominations) and 20% Catholic (2016, *Religious and Public Life*, retrieved from: http://www.pewforum.org/religious-landscape-study/).

I wonder if these people were asked the question, "Are you going to heaven when you die?" … what would their answer be? I suspect it would be, "yes." The question "Based on what?" might produce much more interesting answers. The answers would most likely range from, "I think I'm a good person" to "I believe in a loving God; a loving God wouldn't send anyone to hell."

Maybe even, "I do a lot more good things than I do bad things, so how could I not go to heaven?" Fill in the blank with your answer to this question, and then keep reading to see what the biblical answer is.

Here are the four basic truths about what Christians call salvation. To be "saved" means to have a true relationship with God and to be assured of going to heaven when you die.

Truth #1 God loves you.

Truth #2 You have sinned against God.

Truth #3 God gave us a gift to make us right with Him.

Truth #4 You must believe this and receive this gift in your heart.

Romans 10:9, *If you confess with your mouth Jesus is Lord and believe in your heart that God raised Him from the dead, you will be saved* (NIV).

I believe every person in their lifetime will have an opportunity to accept or reject Jesus Christ as their Lord and Savior (Guaranteeing heaven for your eternity). I'm wondering if this is your opportunity right now. You may say, "I would never reject Jesus Christ," but by not accepting Him and receiving Him, you **are** rejecting Him. **1 John 2:23**, *No one who denies the Son has the Father; whoever acknowledges the Son, has the Father also* (NIV). Please don't make the mistake of not taking the time to understand this critical and universal truth. **John 3:16-18**, *For God so loved the world that He gave His one and only Son that whoever believes in Him shall not perish but have eternal life. For God did not send His Son into the world to condemn the world but save the world through Him. Whoever believes in Him is not condemned, but whoever does not believe stands condemned already, because he has not believed in the name of God's one and only Son* (NIV). I pray for you right now, that the message comes across clearly and is not confusing to you, and that you want to receive Him.

I know in my own life, being raised in a denominational church, I believed all this about God in my head, but not in my heart. I had never "received" the Spirit of God in my heart, which is what is necessary and required. God creates a void in all of us that can only be filled by a true relationship with Him started by receiving the Holy Spirit. We will try to fill that void with any number of things, from money and relationships to sex or work, even "religion." These things are not necessarily bad (in the right context) unless you make them your "god." You know they are your "god" when they "rule" you, when they occupy too much of your time, when you obsess on them… I did on all of the above and the void was still there, waiting to be filled. If you can honestly say that you are fully satisfied and truly content in this life and you don't think you need God, be careful, you will still be judged by Him for what you did in your life. **Hebrews 9:27,** *Just as man is destined once to die and after that to face judgment* (NIV). If you hear me on this matter, continue reading…

The best part of this truth is that God has made it simple to achieve this "spiritual rebirth." You can do it right here and right now by simply saying some words from your heart and believing them to be true. I know some of you may be saying that God cannot accept me because I … (fill in the blank). I live with my girlfriend and we're not married yet. I'm struggling with alcohol, how could God love me? I've done some things in my life that I can't even think about. I've lied and cheated for years about… I've stolen from… Regardless of what you have done, or what you are doing, or what you carry on your shoulders…don't use it as an excuse not to make this decision. God will deal with your baggage later.

The bible deals with this concept as well, in **Philippians 1:6,** *being confident of this that He who began a good work in you will carry it on until completion, until the day of Christ Jesus* (NIV). **You** have to choose to begin that work by receiving Him on His terms and **then** He will guide you through the rest. Are you ready to change your life? Are you ready to give God your heart and watch Him heal you? Do you want a relationship with the maker and creator of all things who has a great plan for your life? Are you ready to receive Him now? Pray these words out loud and mean them in your heart:

Lord God in heaven, I come to you today in Jesus' name. I confess to you that I have sinned against you and I want to repent and receive your forgiveness of sin. I believe in my heart that Jesus died on a cross for the forgiveness of my sin. I believe you raised Him from the dead and I confess with my mouth that Jesus is the Lord of my life and receive your Holy Spirit in my heart right now. Thank you Lord for my salvation, and for eternal life with you in heaven. In Jesus name I pray, Amen.

If you prayed that prayer just now, congratulations. It is a decision you will never regret and a decision you will never forget. Now that you are right with God; now that your **salvation** has been confirmed, let's start learning how to pray **your** "Ultimate Prayer," and discovering God's plan for you. Start praying your "Ultimate Prayer" and find the works that He has prepared for you to do, and you **will** bear fruit. It is an honor, a privilege and blessing like nothing else on earth as you find this in your life.

CHAPTER THREE

BIBLICAL PRAYER TRUTHS

There are hundreds of references to praying in the bible, and it would seem when God speaks about something through His Word hundreds of times, it must be pretty important to Him. This means it should be extremely important to us. Before you create your "Ultimate Prayer," you must look at some truths about praying from God's Word. This will form a foundation on which to build your "Ultimate Prayer."

Truth # 1 God wants us to pray.

1Timothy 2:8, *I want men everywhere to lift up holy hands in prayer* (NIV). It just doesn't get any clearer than that. Sometimes the bible can be interpreted different ways by different people or denominations. People can pull a verse out of context to make a point or even create their own religion. In this case it's pretty straightforward; God wants us to pray, and that should be reason enough for anyone to be motivated to do so. Once we have established that right relationship with Him as discussed in the last chapter, prayer is the next logical step. He will listen! **Ephesians 6:18**, *And pray in the Spirit on all occasions with all kinds of prayers and requests* (NIV). Also in **Psalm 32:6**, *Therefore let everyone who is godly pray to you while you may be found* (NIV). Prayer is communication with God, speaking to Him and listening for Him to speak to you. Any relationship on this earth has to have communication or there is no relationship. The same is true with our relationship with God.

Truth #2 God wants us to pray with each other and for each other.

Soon after Jesus left this earth, His followers gathered together. In **Acts 1:14**, *They all joined together, constantly in prayer, along with the women and Mary, the mother of Jesus, with His brothers* (NIV). The apostle Paul was a huge proponent of praying for others. He wrote in **Ephesians 1:16**, *I have not stopped giving thanks for you, remembering you in my prayers* (NIV).

He states something similar to the believers he wrote to in the book of **Philippians 1:4-6**, *In all my prayers for all of you, I always pray with joy because of your partnership in the gospel from the first day until now, being confident of this, He who began a good work in you will carry it on until completion until the day of Christ Jesus* (NIV). Similarly in the book of **Colossians 1:4**, *We always thank God, the Father of our Lord Jesus Christ when we pray for you* (NIV). And again he demonstrates it in **Ephesians 3:16-17**, *I pray that out of His glorious riches He may strengthen you with power through His Spirit in your inner being, so that Christ may dwell in your hearts through faith* (NIV). There are numerous examples of praying with each other and for each other. We are even to pray for those who mistreat us: **Luke 6:28**, *bless those who curse you, pray for those who mistreat you, and for those who persecute you* (NIV), and in **Matthew 5:44**, *But I tell you: love your enemies and pray for those who persecute you* (NIV). That one takes some real faith.

Truth #3 God wants us to pray civically.

There are times when we are to pray for our city and country. In **Jeremiah 29:7**, *Also seek the peace and prosperity of the city to which I have carried you into exile. Pray to the Lord for it, because if it prospers, you too will prosper* (NIV). Then also in **2 Chronicles 7:14**, *if my people who are called by my name, will humble themselves and pray and seek my face and turn from their wicked ways, then will I hear from* *heaven and will forgive their sin and will heal their land* (NIV). In **Psalm 122:6-8,** *They were instructed to pray for the peace of Jerusalem; May those who love you be secure. May there be peace within your walls and security within your citadels* (NIV). I am certain in these days in which we live, praying for our cities and our country is a great idea. How about praying for our schools and for our elected officials? If just those people lived and ruled us by God's ways, how different could our country look?

Truth #4 God can even help us pray.

As is the case in many things in life, we just don't know where or how to start something. This can happen with our prayer life as well, but not to worry; there is an answer for this, too. In **Romans 8:26,** *In the same way the Spirit helps us in our weakness. We do not know what we ought to pray for, but the Spirit Himself intercedes for us with groans that words cannot express* (NIV). God really loves us and strongly desires a relationship with us. We often don't feel worthy, but even in that mindset, He is there to help.

Truth #5 God's ways are higher than ours.

When we pray, we have to try to comprehend something that borders on the incomprehensible. In **Ephesians 3:20,** *Now to Him who is able to do immeasurably more than we can ask or imagine, according to His power that is at work within us* (NIV). We have to understand that getting what we want is not the purpose of prayer. If God made us, and He did, then God must have a plan for us, and He does. Our mission then, should be to find out what that is, even if it doesn't seem quite right to us at that moment. Think about Jesus Himself in **Matthew 26,** when he showed a hint of humanness by asking God in prayer for something that He would like, but ultimately surrendered to God's will not His own, a perfect example for us. In **Matthew 26:36-42,** *Then Jesus went* with His disciples to a place called Gethsemane, and He said to them, "Sit here while I go over there and pray." He took Peter and the two sons of Zebedee with Him, and He began to be sorrowful and troubled. Then He said to them, "my soul is overwhelmed with sorrow to the point of death. Stay here and keep watch with me." Going a little farther He fell with His face to the ground and prayed, "My Father, if it is possible, may this cup be taken from me. Yet not as I will but as You will." Then He returned to the disciples and found them sleeping. "Could you men not keep watch with me for one hour?" He asked Peter. "Watch and pray that you will not fall into temptation. The spirit is willing but the body is weak." He went away a second time and prayed, "My father, if it is not possible for this cup to be taken away unless I drink it, may Your will be done (NIV)." Jesus prayed and asked, and through this process, determined God's will. The rest is history, thankfully for us.

CHAPTER FOUR

A TIME AND PLACE

Matthew 6:5-6, *And when you pray, do not be like the hypocrites, for they love to pray standing in the synagogue and on the street corners to be seen by men. I tell you the truth; they have received their reward in full. But when you pray, go into your room, close the door and pray to your Father who is unseen. Then your Father who sees what is done in secret will reward you* (NIV).

The most important practice in the "Ultimate" prayer process is making time and finding an appropriate place. This place has to be absolutely free of distractions and noise. Shut off the television, computer and cell phone. If you cannot create this environment, I would use earplugs and a blindfold if necessary, (not kidding). This is about time alone, spent with God; there is nothing more important in your life than investing this time. You have to remember that the enemy and his demons do not want you spending quality time in prayer; it **will** be a battle for you to accomplish this. The biggest obstacle will be distractions. Have you ever really tried to stay focused on one thing without having your brain go in three other directions? Right now, are you even focused on what you're reading here, or are you thinking about what you have to do later or tomorrow? Is your brain telling you that your stomach is a little hungry? Hey! What was that noise? Is the neighbor blowing his leaves on my grass again? …You may still be thinking about the blindfold and earplugs comment! Life is full of distractions. Create an environment to minimize distractions during your "Ultimate Prayer" time and you **will** maximize its effectiveness.

A lot of us have created and sustain such a hectic pace in our daily lives that our brains operate in a constant state of overload. We have a "things to do" list each day that is as long as our arms. Many pride themselves on "multi-tasking." "It's the only way to try to stay on top of things." Most of us worry about things that don't usually end up happening, yet we can't stop thinking about them. The thought of taking some time to pray is hard for some to fathom. Keep your priorities straight! A great example of this is presented in **Luke 10:38-42**, *As Jesus and His disciples were on their way, He came to a village where a woman named Martha opened her home to Him. She had a sister named Mary, who sat at the Lord's feet listening to what He said. But Martha was distracted by all the preparations that had to be made, she came to Him and asked "Lord, don't you care that my sister has left me to do the work by myself? Tell her to help me!" "Martha, Martha," the Lord answered, "you are worried and upset about many things, but only one thing is needed. Mary has chosen what is better and it will not be taken from her* (NIV)." That section of scripture is rich with examples of today's reality. Martha, who had the opportunity to be with Jesus in person got easily distracted; she may have been cleaning up or organizing. Whatever it was, Jesus said she was worried and upset about **many** things (does this sound familiar?). Then He said, "But only one thing is needed!" Her sister chose what was better and He said it would not be taken from her. The lesson here: do not be like Martha, busy and distracted by things that do not matter. Make some uniquely dedicated time and spend it seeking the Lord; it's just better.

In **Hebrews 11:6** it reads, *He rewards those who earnestly seek Him* (NIV). **Proverbs 8:17** reads, *I love those who seek me, and those who seek me find me* (NIV). I think even Jesus realized the importance of a time and a place, as stated in **Matthew 14:23**, *After He dismissed them, He went up on a mountainside by Himself to pray* (NIV). Also in **Matthew 26:38**, *Then Jesus went with His disciples to a place called Gethsemane, and He said to them, "Sit here while I go over there and pray* (NIV)." Now again, please don't misunderstand,

I'm all for prayer groups and praying with your spouse and with your children, praying with others and all such prayer. It is important and necessary. However, the context in which I'm writing this is a little different. This is about you praying to your God, in such a way as to create a deeper level of intimacy, one that I do not believe can be achieved with others or on Sunday at church. By all means go to church and worship, go to church and fellowship, get involved, learn about the bible from your pastor, gain knowledge! But, in **addition** to all of that, formulate your own "Ultimate Prayer."

Finally, your "Ultimate Prayer," as it pertains to "how" you pray. I would suggest to you to say your prayer out loud. Again, your brain is such a busy place and I've always found it easier to at least whisper, if not speak, my personal prayers. When you do this, you are less likely to find yourself thinking about something else. This time you set aside for prayer represents such a small amount of time in your day, make it as high quality as you can. For you numbers people reading, seven minutes of "Ultimate Prayer" time represents less than one half of one percent of your day. Can you afford to set that aside? You can't afford not to.

CHAPTER FIVE

ACKNOWLEDGE AND ASK

Your "Ultimate Prayer" is a personalized prayer, and the personalizing of it begins in this chapter. This book provides you among other things, a template for **your** individual prayer. This chapter is the first phase of how and what you will pray during your "Ultimate Prayer" time. It's here that your journey begins; a journey to seeking God like never before and finding His will for your life. This is the "place" where you will find peace for your mind and rest for your soul. Together, let's go find it!

I love the English language; it's the only one I speak. I never did achieve great grades in English class in high school or college, but I do love looking up words and reading their real definition now (I remember hating it then). I find that I do have a decent vocabulary but I can never quite define a word as well as a dictionary can. When I look up a word, it almost comes alive when I read its full meaning, as the clarity and sometimes the intensity of communication is enhanced. This Chapter is entitled **Acknowledge** and **Ask**. When I looked up the word **Acknowledge** (*www.dictionary.com*, 2016), I was once again amazed.

acknowledge

1.) to admit to be real or true; recognize the existence, truth, or fact of

2.) to show or express recognition or realization of

3.) to recognize the authority, validity, or claims of

4.) to show or express appreciation or gratitude for

5.) to indicate or make known the receipt of

How perfectly these five dictionary definitions apply to our relationship with God through Christ, and confirm and reinforce for me exactly how we should begin a prayer.

We Should Acknowledge Who He Is

Our God is omniscient (all knowing), omnipotent (all powerful), and omnipresent (everywhere always), and somehow He loves us and knows us intimately and individually. **Luke 12:7**, *Indeed, the very hairs of your head are numbered* (NIV). He is the maker and creator: **Colossians 1:15-20**, *He is the image of the invisible God, the firstborn over all creation. For by Him all things were created; things in heaven and on earth, visible and invisible, whether thrones or powers or rulers or authorities; all things were created by Him and for Him. He is before all things, and in Him all things hold together. And He is the head of the body, and the church; He is the beginning and the firstborn among the dead, so that in everything He might have supremacy. For God was pleased to have all His fullness dwell in Him, and through Him to reconcile to Himself all things, whether things on earth or things in heaven, by making peace through His blood, shed on the cross* (NIV). Through this act of Christ on a cross over 2000 years ago, we can have a relationship with Him. Think about this, dwell on this, and come up with your own words to **acknowledge** who He is.

We Should Acknowledge What He Has Made

Genesis 1:1, *In the beginning God created the heavens and the earth* (NIV). There are many beautiful creations on this earth, from mountains and their majesty to the ocean and the creatures therein. I have been blessed to have experienced both of these types of places and as I begin my prayer, I find myself remembering back to the times that I've visited them. Even if you have not been able to see a lot of this earth, surely you've seen pictures or television shows made about it. As you begin to **acknowledge** Him for these creations and the life experiences that you've had or places that you've been, or just things that you've seen, you will find yourself drawing closer to Him. **Acts 17:24,** *The God who made the world and everything in it is the Lord of heaven and earth and does not live in temples built by hands* (NIV). Look around as you live and see what God has made. You don't have to be in church to do this, God is everywhere and you are surrounded by his creations.

We Should Acknowledge What He Has Done

God has reconciled us to Him, allowing us to have a relationship with Him. **2 Corinthians 5:21;** *God made Him who had no sin to be sin for us, so that in Him we might become the righteousness of God* (NIV). Did you read that? We are the righteousness of God! Despite who we are (sinners) and despite who He is (perfectly holy), He still loves us and desires to have a relationship with us. **Isaiah 1:18,** *Come now, let us reason together, says the Lord. Though your sins are like scarlet, they shall be white as snow; though they are red like crimson, they shall be like wool* (NIV). The reason it says "shall be" is… this Old Testament book was created before Christ came to take away your sin. After you have received Christ you can approach God in prayer with a different mindset. **Ephesians 1:4,** *For He chose us in Him before the creation of the world to be holy and blameless in His sight. In love He predestined us to be adopted as sons through Jesus Christ, in accordance with His pleasure and will* (NIV). **Acknowledge** Him for what He has done for you.

We Should Acknowledge Him for Our Access

How awesome it is that we can talk to the God of this universe so immediately and so confidently. **Ephesians 3:12,** *In **Him** and through faith in **Him** we may approach God with freedom and confidence* (NIV). Remember, it's through Christ that we have this access. When this verse refers to '**Him**,' it refers to Christ alone.

This concept is best summarized by the lyrics in one of my all time favorite songs by Casting Crowns.

The song is "Who am I," (2003, Beach Street Records) and the chorus is,

> Not because of who I am
> But because of what You've done.
> Not because of what I've done
> But because of who You are.

To summarize the first phase of your "Ultimate Prayer," personalize the five points above to your own experiences with God and/or incorporate these verses and what they mean to you. Feel free to **acknowledge** Him in your own ways too; **Proverbs 3:5-6,** *Trust in the Lord with all your heart and lean not on your own understanding; in all your ways **acknowledge** Him and He will make your paths straight* (NIV).

We must also **ask** God to hear our prayers. When I looked up the word **ask** *(www.dictionary.com, 2016),*

Ask

    1.) to put a question to

    2.) to request information about

3.) to try to get by using words, request

4.) to solicit from; request of

I believe it an honor and privilege to pray to God; it seems that **asking** comes logically right after **acknowledging. Matthew 7:7-8, *Ask** and it will be given to you, seek and you will find; knock and the door will be opened to you. For everyone who **asks** receives; he who seeks finds; and to him who knocks the door will be opened* (NIV).

Once again to **ask** is not a guarantee of the specific answer that is in your mind. As you read the definitions above you understand that **asking** is just that. **James 1:5,** *If any of you lack wisdom, he should **ask** God, who gives generously to all without finding fault and it will be given to him* (NIV).

God promises in these two verses that you will find and receive, but it's your responsibility to listen and discern **what** He tells you. The promise is… it **will** be given, meaning answers; you will find and it will be opened, meaning understanding. Everyone who **asks** does receive, meaning wisdom. God may say "yes," He may say "no," and He may say "not yet." Be patient. You continue to pray to discern exactly what He is saying to you. Your "Ultimate Prayer" starts like so many other things in life, by **asking** for something. Your life is the result of the decisions you have made. It seems logical to me that we get God's opinion when making important decisions.

Think about how your personal life can change with the simple **asking** of a question…

Will you marry me?

Do you want to buy this house?

How about how our business lives might change…

Can I work for you?

Do you want to start this business together?

How about initiating a spiritual conversation…

Do you believe in God?

Are you a religious person?

Big things can happen in this life when we **ask** questions. Bigger things can happen now and eternally when we **ask** questions of our Heavenly Father. Go ahead, ***ask*** *Him*.

CHAPTER SIX

CONFESS AND REPENT

Phase 2 of your "Ultimate Prayer" deals with **confession** and **repentance**. Quite often I think the devil uses guilt to keep us from praying to the Lord. In many "religious" circles, guilt is used in ways that disrupt the process of prayer, not to mention your own self image and self confidence. In your own mind you may say, "Who am I that I can pray to God?" "I think the priest or pastor is supposed to do that." Many of us feel unworthy or inadequate, insufficient or just lacking somehow, and prayer never happens, spiritual growth never happens, intimacy with God never happens. This can lead to a life of routines, stagnation and boredom; even worse, it can send you into a downward spiral leading to despair and ending in depression. God does not want this for your life!

In the process of creating your own "Ultimate Prayer," the issue of sin must still be dealt with, to give you the freedom and confidence to pray. This starts with **confessing** your sin, **1 John 1:9**, *If we **confess** our sins He is faithful and just and will forgive our sins and purify us from all unrighteousness* (NIV).

con·fess

1.) to declare or acknowledge (one's sins), especially to God or a priest in order to obtain absolution (*www.dictionary. com*, 2016)

re·pent

> 1.) to feel sorry or contrite for past conduct; regret or conscience-stricken (*www.dictionary.com*, 2016)

> 2.) to feel sorrow for sin or fault as to be disposed to change one's life for the better; to be penitent (*www.dictionary.com*, 2016)

Acts 3:19, *Repent* *then, and turn to God, so that your sins may be wiped out, that times of refreshing may come from the Lord* (NIV). Through this process of **confessing** and **repenting**, your mind should be in a place to move forward in your "Ultimate Prayer," because the truth of the matter as written in His word is this, **Hebrews 8:12,** *For I will forgive their wickedness and remember their sins no more* (NIV). Once again, a holy God cannot have a relationship with a sinful man. He gives us a way to deal with this that is final and complete. **Jeremiah 5:19a,** *Therefore this is what the Lord says: If you **repent** I will restore you that you might serve me* (NIV).

You must rid yourself of guilt to be able to receive from the Lord. You have no guilt if you do what His word says. **Colossians 2:13,** *When you were dead in your sins and in the uncircumcision of your sinful nature, God made you alive with Christ, **He forgave us all our sins*** (NIV). Many will struggle with accepting these truths in their minds. This does not change the fact that it is the truth, **Ephesians 1:7-8,** *In Him we have redemption through His blood, the forgiveness of sins in accordance with the riches of God's grace* (NIV). Regardless of what you have done in your life, there is forgiveness in Christ and as we **confess** and **repent**, He can redirect our life paths. **Isaiah 1:18,** *Come let us reason together says the Lord, though your sins are like scarlet, they shall be white as snow, though they are red as crimson they shall be like wool* (NIV). During this second phase of your "Ultimate Prayer," you must receive His full forgiveness. If you still struggle in this area, buy a bible with a concordance. A concordance shows you where a particular word is used in the bible. For example, in my bible, the words forgive and forgiveness are used in 95 different places. Are you struggling with something? Look it up in a concordance and see what *God's word* says about it. Your opinion might change.

Through the **confessing** of your sins and the **repenting** of your sins, you are put in a position of favor and right standing with the Lord. In summary, after starting your "Ultimate Prayer" by **acknowledging** and **asking**, you must next **confess** and **repent**.

CHAPTER SEVEN

THANKSGIVING AND PRAISE

Phase 3 of your "Ultimate Prayer" consists of you giving **thanksgiving** and **praise** to our Lord. **Ephesians 5:20,** *always giving* **thanks** *to God the father for everything, in the name of our Lord Jesus Christ* (NIV). Each of these phases of your prayer is designed to prepare you for the next. You started with **Acknowledging** and **Asking**, you then **Confessed** and **Repented**, and now you are giving **Thanksgiving** and **Praise**. Once again, I use a dictionary definition of these terms to drive home the real meaning of these words.

thanks·giv·ing

1.) the act of giving **thanks**; grateful acknowledgement of benefits or favors, especially to God (*www.dictionary. com*, 2016)

2.) an expression of **thanks**, especially to God (*www.dictionary. com*, 2016)

3.) a public celebration in acknowledgement of divine favor or kindness (*www.dictionary.com*, 2016)

praise

1.) the act of expressing approval or admiration; commendation; laudation *(www.dictionary.com, 2016)*

2.) the offering of grateful homage in words or song, as an act of worship: *a hymn of **praise** to God (www.dictionary. com, 2016)*

This **thanksgiving** and **praise** section of your prayer should help you to transcend what you're thinking or feeling. During this particular aspect of prayer time, we are following **Colossians 3:2**, *Set your minds on things above, not earthly things* (NIV). This is definitely God's will for you as stated in the bible.

1 Thessalonians 5:18, *give **thanks** in all circumstances, for this is God's will for you in Christ Jesus* (NIV). I firmly believe that as a person thinks, so will he be (**Proverbs 23:7**).

As you give **thanks** and **praise** you become **thankful**, and your whole mindset, your whole attitude can change. Once again, the bible gives us repeated direction to do certain things, and to do these things involves a conscious decision on your part. When you think about these things, and dwell on such thoughts, He **will** change your "earthly" thoughts and turn them into "heavenly" thoughts. **Romans 12:2**, *Do not conform any longer to the patterns of this world but be transformed by the renewing of your mind* (NIV). When you spend hours each day watching television or surfing the 'net reading various articles or listening to the radio, you are in fact being conformed to this world. It's difficult to see God or think about Him. In all likelihood, you need some transcending of your thoughts and some renewing of your mind. Don't wait until Sunday to do this, take a few minutes each day and watch Him change you for good. **Colossians 3:17**, *And whatever you do, whether in word or deed, do it all in the name of the Lord Jesus, giving **thanks** to God the Father through Him* (NIV).

Over and over again the sentiment of **thanksgiving** and **praise** is spoken. **Hebrews 13:15**, *Through Jesus therefore, let us continually offer to God a sacrifice of **praise** - the fruit of lips that confess His name* (NIV). The third part of your "Ultimate Prayer" should really prepare you to seek God. Giving **thanksgiving** and **praise** is something that should come easily regardless of your circumstances. Despite the fact that there are many challenges in this life, you can still find things to be **thankful** for. If you're having a difficult time, read **Psalm 100**, it's just five verses but it will get you started.

You may be **thankful** for your wife or husband, for your kids or grandkids...family is often a good place to start. You may be **thankful** for your health, vision, hearing, taste... You may be **thankful** for a friend or your church. How about being **thankful** for a relationship with God, or how He sees you? **1 Peter 2:9**, *But you are a chosen people, a royal priesthood, a holy nation, a people belonging to God, that you may declare the **praises** of Him who called you out of darkness and into His wonderful light* (NIV). That verse is most worthy of **thankfulness**. The bottom line - when you find yourself focusing on things to be **thankful** for, your attitude will change and your thoughts will be in a better place, which will bring you to a better place. This will also lead you to the final phase of **your** "Ultimate Prayer."

CHAPTER EIGHT

SEEK, SEARCH, BE STILL & LISTEN

This is the most important chapter in this entire book. It is Phase 4 in the creation of your "Ultimate Prayer," the final step, the final part; it will all come together here. It is in this chapter that you will reach the culmination of your "Ultimate Prayer" process. It is here that you will **seek** the Lord, having **acknowledged** and **asked**, having **confessed** and **repented**, having given **thanks** and **praise** - the groundwork has been laid down. It is now time to **seek, search, be still** and **listen. Jeremiah 42:3**, *Pray that the Lord your God will tell us where we should go and what we should do* (NIV).

I live in South Florida in an area designated a bird sanctuary. I see some cool creations of God in "their" environment. There are many birds, including Ibis, Egrets, and Great Blue Herons to name a few. The other day I watched a Heron, and it reminded me of this chapter. He was standing on the shoreline of a lake; silent and focused he stood motionless. He was **seeking** a place; moments later he took a few steps and stopped while his eyes seemed to **search** the clear waters below. Several minutes went by and yet he remained absolutely motionless, **still**, like a statue. I am certain he was **listening.** Finally, without warning he struck! He was rewarded for following the steps with which God had innately equipped him to meet his needs. God has equipped us to meet our needs, but we don't always follow the steps to find them. I reiterate the main foundational verse of this book, **Ephesians 2:10**, *For we are God's workmanship created in Christ Jesus to do good works which God prepared for us to do* (NIV).

When you arrive at this point in the creation of your "Ultimate Prayer," where you have prayed about **acknowledging** and **asking**, prayed about **confessing** and **repenting**, prayed about giving **thanks** and **praise**, you are positioned to pray about **seeking, searching, being still** and **listening**. **Jeremiah 29:12-13**, *Then you will call upon me and come and pray to me, and I will listen to you. You will seek me and find me when you seek me with all your heart* (NIV). Your mind should be in a great place to receive. Receive what? Receive answers about the things that are on your heart. Receive discernment on where to go and what to do. Receive wisdom on how to handle a situation. Receive knowledge that you need to have, receive understanding about why something did or did not happen, receive strength to continue, receive knowledge of God's will for you... This is where your "Ultimate Prayer" really gets personalized. I don't know where you are in life. I don't know what you're going through. I do know this; everyone I've ever met on this earth has had to endure valleys to get to mountain tops. You know you can't see a rainbow without rain. So, whether you are old or young, a new believer who is just opening the bible or a deacon in a church for 40 years...whether you're married, single, widowed or a divorced person, or someone going through loss or divorce right now, you need prayer. You may be someone with a lot of money or someone with none, you may have struggled with substance abuse or have never taken an aspirin, you may have no kids or eight of them and you need prayer. God answers prayer.

Do you believe He answers prayer? I believe God answers prayers, sometimes with a 'Yes,' sometimes with a 'No,' and many times with a 'Wait' answer. This too can be determined in this phase of your "Ultimate Prayer." Keep this in mind, however, 'Yes' does not necessarily mean this minute, 'No' does not mean never, and 'Wait' may mean you are not ready, or patience is required here.

When it comes to answers to prayer, you must understand and accept **Isaiah 55:8-9**, *For my thoughts are not your thoughts, neither are your ways my ways declares the Lord. As the heavens are higher than* *the earth, so are my ways higher than your ways and my thoughts higher than your thoughts* (NIV). The real purpose of all of this is to work your way through things in life, good and bad. We know this life will give us trials, God allows it for a purpose. In **John 16:33**, *In this world you will have trouble. But take heart! I have overcome the world* (NIV). Keep believing, keep praying, and as you do, you will get answers. They may not always seem right, or even the answers you want, but if prayed through thoroughly, they will be the answers that are best for you. **James 1:6**, *But when he asks, he must believe and not doubt, because he who doubts is like a wave of the sea, blown and tossed by the wind* (NIV). During this critical phase of your "Ultimate Prayer," **seek, search, be still** and **listen**. Most of your time during the four phases of your "Ultimate Prayer" will most likely be spent here. Don't take the first three lightly but it is here that you will be led into God's will for your life.

CHAPTER NINE

PUTTING YOUR "ULTIMATE PRAYER" TOGETHER

I hope that in the writings of the past four chapters, you have considered the creation of your own personalized "Ultimate Prayer," which I hope will lead you to places in your relationship with God through Christ that you've never been, maybe that you could never even fathom. This will take time to achieve. It will evolve as the Spirit leads, and requires some meditating on the scriptures that inspired this whole book and concept. Be patient with this, as I'm sure God has been patient with you in your life. As a final way of helping you with this process, I thought I would provide you with an example of an "Ultimate Prayer." Its template should resemble yours, but you'll see how the personalized part can be customized and interchanged to meet your own situation and circumstances. Also, I believe in pauses... As you read through the "Ultimate Prayer" sample below, each '...' represents an opportunity to **pause, seek, search, be still** and **listen**, and possibly consider or personalize your "Ultimate Prayer." Throughout your prayer, simply allow the Holy Spirit to work through your mind and heart and even lead and guide your prayer, especially in the fourth phase where you are **seeking, searching, being still** and **listening**. This too will develop as you continue on this journey.

My "Ultimate Prayer" (sample):

Heavenly Father, Lord Jesus, Holy Spirit, I thank you for this time of prayer and I <u>ask</u> you in your name to receive it... I <u>acknowledge</u> you as the Lord and Savior of my life and believe that you are the maker and creator of this earth and all that is in it. I <u>acknowledge</u> that you are omniscient, omnipotent and omnipresent and that you are alive and active on this earth and in my life. I believe that you are the God of Abraham, Isaac and Jacob, the God of Israel, and the God of America. I believe in you Lord and lift up my prayers to you today... Help me to understand more about who you are, what you are doing and what you have done. I <u>acknowledge</u> that you, Lord Jesus, walked this earth and lived a sinless life, according to God's will, only to voluntarily give your life as a ransom for so many. I believe in you Jesus, all that you are and all that you have done. I believe the Holy Spirit lived in and through you, that very Spirit that we receive upon our <u>acknowledgement</u> of you for the forgiveness of our sins. That Spirit is at work through all who believe and accept you; all who have received you. I <u>acknowledge</u> that you willingly took the punishment for my sin on a cross that day you died Lord, only to rise again, and you are now seated at the right hand of God. You were beaten and tortured, yet you did not stop them, even though you had the power to do so, until your final words, "it is finished."

I <u>confess</u> Lord, that I am a sinner and that I have sinned. I know I will sin again; I always want to do as your word says Lord, but you know I still live in this fallen world and in this flesh. Help me to <u>repent</u> and turn from my sins. Your word says that you are faithful and will forgive me as I <u>confess and repent</u>. Your word says if I <u>confess</u> with my mouth and believe in my heart, then I will be saved. I thank you for salvation, for allowing me to have a relationship with you. I do not deserve it Lord, but I <u>thank</u> you with all my heart for it. Great are you Lord and worthy of <u>praise</u>... so I <u>praise</u> you and your holy name.

My thankfulness seems so small and weak when I think about all that you've done for me, the heaven that you promised me Lord, when I think about streets of gold and a place without sin and most importantly a place where you are there with me. I can't comprehend exactly what that will be like Lord, but I thank you for it and praise you that you will allow me to be there despite what I've done in my life. Thank you that my sins, though they are red as scarlet, are now white as snow. They are as far as East is from West. I thank you for your grace and mercies, which are new each day. I thank you for your word, the ability to read it, and understand it. I thank you for the opportunity to worship you and even to pray to you. I thank you for the relationship that you allow me to have with you. I thank you for my church, family, friends and health. I thank you for freedom. I thank you for my life.

Now Lord I want to seek you with all my heart. I surrender all to you and pray that you will fill me with your Holy Spirit; I want to make myself available to you to be used however you wish. You are the vine and I am the branch. Apart from you, I can do nothing. Your word says that I am God's workmanship created in Christ Jesus to do good works, which you prepared for me. I ask that you guide me into these works, for if you do, I know they will be fruitful. Nothing is more satisfying deep down than to be used by you in the lives of people. I pray for discernment and for wisdom on these matters. I pray for sensitivity to your Holy Spirit. Help me to perceive, help me to discern what you are leading me to do. Help me to stay out of your way and just allow you to flow through me. I know your word is a light for my feet, a lamp for my path; help me to absorb your word like a sponge, that you would wring me out onto others in a Spirit led way. Help me to just draw close to you. Help me to find your will for my life. I want to honor you and glorify you through my words, my attitude, and my actions every day in every way. I am not capable of this in my own strength and power but I know that Christ in me is capable of all these things and more.

I want to <u>seek</u> you today and every day, Lord. Specifically, I pray for my relationship with you, Lord. I ask that you reveal to me and convict me if there's something in my life that I am doing that is wrong or sinful in your sight that I am not aware of... or something that I'm not doing that I should be... Speak to my heart I humbly ask in these areas... I ask you Lord to increase my faith, help me to grow in the knowledge of who I am in Christ, and how Christ is in me... I pray for direction in my life with regard to serving you, and where you would have me do this... How can I do this...? I always want to be available to be used by you in the lives of the people you put in my path. Thank you for this blessing and honor.

I pray for my family...(you individualize this as things arise and change...).

I pray for my finances, my work, and for stewardship of what you've given me... (you individualize this so it is specific to you...).

I pray for my fitness, my health, and the physical ability to be able to continue to do all that you have called me to do and all that I am responsible for here, Lord...

I pray for your healing hand upon my physical body and my mind; cleanse me Lord from my past...

Help me to <u>be still</u> and <u>listen</u> now Lord, and hear your still small voice. Help me discern your will for my life in these areas... Speak to me Lord about who I can pray for and how... Speak to me Lord if there is an area or direction I should be moving toward, or one I should be running from... Please lead, guide and direct my paths in this life with your wisdom. Help me to <u>listen</u> and to pray for a special sensitivity to your Holy Spirit in me...

It is in the Holy and precious name of Jesus that I pray...Amen.

CHAPTER TEN

GOD'S WILL FOR SURE

MATTHEW 7:13-14, *ENTER through the narrow gate. For wide is the gate and broad is the road that leads to destruction and many enter through it. But small is the gate and narrow the road that leads to life and only a few find it* (NIV).

As a person who has received Jesus Christ as Lord and Savior, as one who now has the Holy Spirit living in and through them, and finally as one who is praying your own "Ultimate Prayer," you are in a unique place; you are on the narrow road as described in the verse above. You are positioned to find God's desired will for your life and you've actually taken the first few steps! **Psalm 143:10,** *Teach me to do your will for you are my God; may your good Spirit lead me on level ground* (NIV). It is now your mission, and you now have many tools to discover it. This will be a very individual exploration. God does have a plan for you! It was said to the Israelites in the Old Testament this way... **Jeremiah 29:11-14,** *For I know the plans I have for you declares the Lord, plans to prosper you and to not harm you, plans to give you hope and a future. Then you will call upon me and come and pray to me, and I will listen to you. You will seek me and find me when you seek me with all your heart. I will be found by you declares the Lord, and bring you back from captivity* (NIV). I understand that this was written to the "believers" back then, but you are a believer today and it's just as appropriate to you today as it was then. The captivity that He will bring you back from is your own "junk," your own "stuff," meaning your struggles, issues, problems and sins. Like it or not, realize it or not, believe it or not, if you live on this earth, you are most likely in some form of captivity. You simply cannot achieve victory over it and escape from it without some serious prayer. It's the only way you have to communicate with Him and allow Him to do this work in you and help you achieve victory over it. It's not just to get you through these things, important as that is, but to help you to do what He has planned for you to do, His desired will for you. This is true for each one of us. As He clears out the "old" He makes room for the new, **2 Corinthians 5:17**, *Therefore, if anyone is in Christ, the new creation has come: The old has gone, the new is here!* (NIV). Again, I quote **Ephesians 2:10**, *For we are God's workmanship created in Christ Jesus to do good works which God prepared for us to do* (NIV). He wants to lead you and guide you into this, and promises to do so. **Psalm 32:8**, *I will instruct you and teach you in the way you should go; I will counsel you and watch over you* (NIV). To assist you in discerning this, I have created a section at the end of this book for you to write things down that you discover through this prayer process. This prayer journal will allow you to write down the things that you experience and receive in your journey. Specific dates that you will look back on and remember what God did for you, what He allowed you to experience and why. Remember this, **Romans 8:28**, *And we know that in all things God works for the good of those who love Him, who have been called according to His purpose* (NIV). This journal might provide something to share with others to encourage and strengthen them. It might be used later in your own life as you recall what God did "back then" and give **you** the faith "now" …the possibilities are endless. I encourage you to fill in this section and review it from time to time.

In **1Timothy 6:20**, *Paul said to Timothy, guard what has been entrusted to your care* (NIV). I say to you today the same, not only guard but take seriously when you feel the Spirit is placing someone or something on your heart. God has a plan for that person or that thing too, and by writing it in this journal and being consistent and persistent in praying about it, you will determine His will about it.

Having said all this, there are certain aspects of God's will that apply to all of us. There is God's "general" will for all of us (these can help you determine God's specific will for you "individually"). When you read **Matthew: 7:21**, *Not everyone who says to me "Lord, Lord" will enter the kingdom of heaven, but only he who does the will of my Father who is in heaven* (NIV). It should be our number one desire to find and do His will. Jesus Himself demonstrated this very objective in **John 6:38**, *For I have come down from heaven not to do my will but to do the will of Him who sent me…* (NIV). With that in mind, here are a few examples of God's general will for all of us.

Acts 2:38, *Peter replied, "Repent and be baptized. Every one of you, in the name of Jesus Christ for the forgiveness of your sins. And you will receive the Holy Spirit* (NIV).

1Timothy 2:3-4, *This is good, and pleases God our savior, who wants all men to be saved and come to a knowledge of the truth* (NIV).

1 Thessalonians 5:12-18, *Now we ask you, brothers, to respect those who work hard among you, who are over you in the Lord and who admonish you. Hold them in the highest regard in love because of their work. Live in peace with each other. And we urge you, brothers, warn those who are idle, encourage the timid, help the weak, be patient with everyone. Make sure that nobody pays back wrong for wrong but always try to be kind to each other and everyone else. Be joyful always; pray continually; give thanks in all circumstances, for this is God's will for you in Christ Jesus* (NIV).

Ephesians 5:16-20, *Be very careful then how you live, making the most of every opportunity, because the days are evil. Therefore do not be foolish, but understand what the Lord's will is. Do not be drunk on wine, which leads to debauchery. Instead be filled with the Spirit. Speak to one another with psalms, hymns and spiritual songs. Sing and make* *music in your heart to the Lord, always giving thanks to God the father for everything, in the name of our Lord Jesus Christ* (NIV).

1 Thessalonians 4:3-6, *It is **God's will** that you should be sanctified: that you should avoid sexual immorality; that each of you should learn to control his own body in a way that is holy and honorable, not in the passionate lust like the heathen, who do not know God; and in this matter no one should wrong his brother or take advantage of him...* (NIV).

These are just a few examples of many where God shows us His **will for sure**. As you read through the bible, look for more of these types of verses.

Another aspect of **God's will for sure** has to do with the fruits of the Spirit. **Galatians 5:22-23**, *But the fruit of the spirit is love, joy, peace, patience, kindness, goodness, faithfulness, gentleness and self control* (NIV). By "fruit" of the spirit it means the result of or consequence of, the outcome of or the end product of... this is what is to flow from you or come out of you as a Christian because it's not you per se, it's the Spirit in you (or literally through you). Of course we still live in the "flesh" and in a world that has another god. That god is described in **Ephesians 2:1-2**, *As for you, you were dead in your transgressions and sins, in which you used to live when you followed the ways of this world and the ruler of the kingdom of the air, the spirit who is now at work in those who are disobedient* (NIV). This is not God, this is the devil. The same spirit as described in **2 Corinthians 4:4**, *The god of this age has blinded the minds of the unbelievers, so that they cannot see the glory of Christ who is the image of God* (NIV). By the way, this god has fruits too! The outcome of...or result of...that spirit leading you and "living" through you? They are listed in **Galatians 5:19-21**, *The acts of the sinful nature are obvious: sexual immorality, impurity and debauchery; idolatry and witchcraft; hatred, discord, jealousy, fits of rage, selfish ambitions, dissensions, factions and envy; drunkenness, orgies, and the like. I warn you as I did before, that those who live like this will not inherit the kingdom of heaven* (NIV). So here is a great compare and contrast situation. Which list of "fruits" would you rather produce in your life? **God's will for sure** should be obvious. Use your "Ultimate Prayer" to find His **will** for you, specifically, but read His word and see His **will** for all of us when we surrender and allow Him to flow through us.

You must endeavor to accomplish this in a consistent, patient and real way. **Hebrews 10:22**, *let us draw near to God with a sincere heart* (NIV). When you do this He will literally transform you from the inside out. Again I will quote **Romans 12:2**, *Do not conform any longer to the pattern of this world, but be transformed by the renewing of your mind. Then you will be able to test and approve what God's will is - His good, pleasing and perfect will* (NIV)**.** This is where the excitement begins. When you discover **His will for you**, these "works" he has planned, and you pray about pursuing them and implementing them; when you start **doing** them, this is where that deep satisfaction, that feeling that no drug will ever give you, that sense of God working through YOU is found. You are going to like that… It will create thoughts, feelings and emotions probably unfamiliar to you, but amazingly satisfying. The words epiphany and catharsis come to my mind. This is the point… the purpose of this book… the reason for your life on this earth… pursue it! Prayerfully, of course…

Surely now, you have figured out that God's word, the Holy Bible, is the basis for this book. In **Mark 13:31**, *Heaven and earth will pass away but my word will never pass away* (NIV). In **Psalm 119:105**, *Your word is a lamp to my feet and a light for my path* (NIV). **Hebrews 4:12**, *The word of God is living and active. Sharper than any double-edged sword, it penetrates even dividing soul and spirit, joints and marrow; it judges the thoughts and attitudes of the heart* (NIV). Personally, I am continually adding "memory verses" to my mental collection. I believe that the more of God's word that is memorized, the more you become like a sponge that is filled with refreshing life-giving water. You have a greater opportunity to be wrung out on someone who is dry, thirsty and in need of such refreshment

(Please don't drown them). **John 7:37-38,** *On the last and greatest day of the festival, Jesus stood and said in a loud voice, "Let anyone who is thirsty come to me and drink. Whoever believes in me, as Scripture has said, rivers of living water will flow from within them..."* (NIV). Sharing God's word with others is definitely part of **God's will for sure** for your life. To whom, when, what and where should be discerned through your prayer time (It is better to bear fruit, not to bruise it). With this in mind, I encourage you to pray for availability, discernment and **then,** boldness... I also suggest you pray for sensitivity to the Holy Spirit in each circumstance. **2 Timothy 3:16-17,** *All scripture is God-breathed and is useful for teaching and rebuking, correcting and training in righteousness, so that the man of God may be thoroughly equipped for every good work* (NIV).

When praying to God, bible verses quite often form prayers. They are certainly a part of prayers, and are incorporated into many prayers. Sometimes meditating on certain verses will send you in a different direction, one that may be a direction in which He would want you to head off. Sometimes verses will lead you in a direction in which He would want you to move, again praying for discernment or sometimes confirmation will help you understand the difference. Occasionally, others may tell you about a verse that the Lord gave them recently, and maybe He gave it to them to give to you! It may serve to encourage you, caution you, direct you or confirm an idea. He may have given you a verse for someone else. This all will be discerned in the **seeking** and **searching** section of your "Ultimate Prayer." With this in mind, I have placed a section at the end of this book specifically focused on the memorization of scripture. I've chosen some areas and topics that seem especially relevant in today's society. Many of these verses are on my personal memorization list and may just make it to yours! Although they might not apply to you or your life today, they may be helpful to someone that God has placed in your path, not by coincidence but by His sovereignty, so that you can be used to make an impact. Really, His word through you to change someone's life, and again, as much as they are changed through His power, you get blessed knowing His Spirit has just flowed through YOU! I've also left some blank pages for you to add your own verses to memorize. Challenge yourself!

Need some additional motivation? Think about scripture memorization this way. How is it that you know the words to rock and roll songs from 10, 20 or even 30 years ago, and you don't know more than a few bible verses? Here's a test, Can you finish this musical lyric? "I can't get no" …(satisfaction)… How about, "…and she's buying a stairway to" …(heaven)… I'm sure, depending on your age, you could sing dozens of your favorite songs or more from memory. I don't think it'll do much for your relationship with God, fun as it may be; it might just remind you of a time that you lived apart from Him. …My suggestion? **Memorize God's word**. You may just find yourself in a position to use it – with a stranger or a friend or even the battlefield of your own mind. There are over 150 verses in this book. Pick one each week and start using the memory verse journal in the back of this book. Watch God provide an opportunity for you to use them.

One of the many reasons to pray is to work your way through all the information that comes in through your eyes, ears and brain each day. The information comes in at such a rate it's amazing we can process it. I think it causes a system overload and creates an inability for us to focus. As crazy as it sounds, I will count the number of times images change in a 30 second commercial on television. I don't know what the actual average is, but quite often it's 30 or more times (Yes, I have counted)! One commercial, one time… how many commercials are there in an hour of television? So much information is communicated each day, and before you know it, you're brainwashed. "15 minutes can save you 15% or more on…" …have you seen or heard that one before? Can you finish that statement? This reinforces why you should take time each day to **seek, search, be still** and **listen** to things that **really matter**, and get that plethora of competing things that really don't matter set aside in your mind. Only then can you get focused on something that might actually change your day... your life... and your world, and maybe better yet, someone else's.

I've read that our brain is more powerful than any computer ever made; this God-given object is a powerful tool, but also a potentially dangerous one. Do you ever have a hard time shutting off your brain? Can you ever not go to sleep at night? Is it because your mind is going a hundred different directions? Can you just not stop thinking sometimes? Be honest with yourself, think about some of the thoughts you've had even today; anything Weird? Strange? Scary? Illegal? Sinful? Where do these thoughts come from? Welcome to reality. Welcome to the battlefield of the mind. Of course amazingly, God knew all of this and He has given us help for this battle. Start by admitting to yourself, the old adage that denial is not just a river in Egypt...and take steps to achieve victory and peace of mind. It's described and illustrated in **Ephesians 6:12-17**, *For our struggle is not against flesh and blood, but against the rulers, against the authorities, against the powers of this dark world and against the spiritual forces of evil in the heavenly realms. Therefore put on the full armor of God, so that when the day of evil comes, you may be able to stand your ground, and after you have done everything, to stand. Stand firm then, with the belt of truth buckled around your waist, with the breastplate of righteousness in place, and with your feet fitted with the readiness that comes from the gospel of peace. In addition to all this, take up the shield of faith, with which you can extinguish all the flaming arrows of the evil one. Take the helmet of salvation and the sword of the Spirit which is the word of God* (NIV). Praying this armor to be "on you" is **God's will for sure**, for you to win these battles in your mind against an enemy that you cannot see but yet is very real. By memorizing scripture verses and using them in this process, by journaling the events, I truly believe you will win the battle and live in His grace and in victory, achieving the "peace that transcends all understanding" (**Philippians 4:7**). This, for you, is **God's will for sure.**

CLOSING

The subtitle of this book is "7 minutes to change your day...your life...and your world." As I begin closing, I'd like to share some final thoughts. I thought I would share my dream for this venture, my vision for it, and my sincere hope. I truly pray that you can see my vision, share in my dream, and actually become a part of it...

Have you ever gotten involved in a network marketing company, sometimes called a multi-level marketing company? The premise is pretty simple. If you could just find three people to purchase this product and help them each find three people to also purchase this product, then teach them and help them to get three people to each purchase this product and so on... The numbers go from one person, you, to 729 in just six cycles, and jump to over a half million in the next six cycles of this math pyramid. Then you go to local meetings, then regional meetings and eventually, national meetings. Motivational speakers are brought in to get people "pumped up" to go home and get more people, and on and on. All this for the sake of money... Oh, they'll tell you it's about people, and I suppose it's possible that some friendships could be made through this process, but I know it's money driven. They'll show you pictures of people in huge houses, on yachts, driving fancy sports cars and in places with beaches, blue water and palm trees, "living the dream," and you can too! I understand that money is necessary in this life; I would even say I like having money, but just remember, the bible says that the LOVE of it is the root of all evil (**1Timothy 6:10**). Before I accepted Christ in my life, I tried a multi-level marketing company and saw some of this first hand, even the "friends" part, until these "friends" realized you just wanted to be friends, and not push their product, and then they seemed to only spend time with the "friends" who **did** push their product. After I became a Christian I dabbled with a different network marketing company and even asked God to bless my efforts with this product and business. Then the Spirit spoke to my heart. I realized I was putting more effort into this product and business than I was into telling people about God and what He could do for them, what He has done for me, and I felt like that was the last time I would ever be involved with a pyramid company. To this day, it has been the case. My opinion? Get involved in something that has eternal ramifications, something that can really change someone's life for good, or change this world, forever. I envision options opening to accomplish this when you pray your "Ultimate Prayer."

I recently read an article about lottery winners in this country, how many of them ended up financially bankrupt after becoming millionaires. The numbers are astounding. Every week when I go to the grocery store I see people lined up to buy their tickets for the lottery, (with the same dream those multi-level marketing people have). Maybe we should introduce them to some of those "winners" who have lost it all, or maybe we could just tell them about Christ and the riches that he has for us. This is my hope.

For clarification purposes I feel I need to explain a very important fact. Your "Ultimate Prayer" is not the only way to pray, it's not the only time that you should pray, and it's not to be a limit to your prayers. If you have a relationship with someone on this earth, and they wake up in your home, you would say good morning to them. When you first see a business acquaintance or a neighbor, there is a greeting that soon follows. With these earthly relationships there are various levels of intimacy with which come various types of greetings. When you truly understand the relationship you have with God Almighty, starting every day you wake up with a prayer of thanks seems appropriate.

Ending every day with a prayer of thanks also seems appropriate. The food provision that you receive each day seems worthy of thanks. There are so many things to be praying about, people to be praying for and with, churches, schools and ministries to be praying for. Don't let your "Ultimate Prayer" time be the only time you pray. In America, we take a great deal for granted, but don't let our abundance keep you from giving thanks to God. Even short prayers throughout your day can keep you Christ-centered and sensitive to the Holy Spirit in and around you. You may have heard of a "Nehemiah prayer." In the second chapter of the book of Nehemiah, he was about to ask of a king a huge request. I am sure he had been praying about this for some time (as stated in chapter 1 of Nehemiah), but look what happens: **Nehemiah 2:4**, *The king said to me "What is it you want?" Then I prayed to the God of heaven and I answered the king* (NIV). Take note that he asked God before proceeding. Take time throughout your day, regardless of how much time you have to do it, and pray. It shows your desire for an intimate relationship with God. He will hear your prayer.

And finally… One of my favorite musical artists, Steven Curtis Chapman, released a song entitled *"Heaven in the Real World"* (1994, Sparrow Records) with an excerpt from a Chuck Colson speech which seems even more relevant today than it was over 20 years ago when it was spoken. Chuck said, "Where is the hope? I meet millions who tell me they feel demoralized by the decay around them. Where is the hope? The hope that each of us has is not in who governs us or what laws are passed or what great things we do as a nation, our hope is in the power of God working through the hearts of people; that's where our hope is in this country, that's where our hope is in life."

This captures the essence of the "Ultimate Prayer," the power of God working through the hearts of people. There are so many things that could be done for good if we catch that vision. There are so many things that have been done because people have prayed and been faithful to that vision that God gave them. God wants to use you to do something special, something that you were made by Him to do. Make it your mission in life to discover what that is. No one has the unique personality formed by your life experience, be it good or bad, by your family upbringing, be it good or bad. No one has your unique educational experience, be it formal or from "street smarts, the school of hard knocks." God is sovereign and knew all of this about you, and wants you to use it all in ministering to others... and the best part of it all? You will be as blessed as they are because you are right where you are supposed to be, in the middle of **God's will for your life**.

Surrender your life and find out what God will do through you. Nothing will be more satisfying, I promise.

In closing this book, I want to say thank you for reading my "Christian experience," and I want to pray for you the prayer that Paul prayed for the people in Ephesus.

Ephesians 3:14-19: *For this reason I kneel before the Father, from whom His whole family in heaven and on earth derives its name. I pray that out of His glorious riches He may strengthen you with power through His Spirit in your inner being, so that Christ may dwell in your hearts through faith. And I pray that you, being rooted and established in love, may have power, together with all the saints, to grasp how wide and long and high and deep is the love of Christ, and to know this love that surpasses knowledge – that you may be filled to the measure of all the fullness of God. Now to Him who is able to do immeasurably more than all we ask or imagine, according to His power that is at work within us, to Him be the glory in the church and in Christ Jesus throughout all generations, forever and ever! Amen* (NIV).

Visit www.ultimateprayerbook.com and join us in sharing your personal "Ultimate Prayer" story.

SCRIPTURE MEMORIZATION

Anxiety

Matthew 6:25-27

_____
_____
_____

Philippians 4:6-7

_____
_____
_____

1 Peter 5:6-7

_____
_____
_____

Psalm 34: 4

_____
_____
_____

Comfort

Matthew 11:28

_____
_____
_____

Roman 8:28

_____
_____
_____

Psalm 55:22

_____
_____
_____

2Corinthians 1:3-4

_____
_____
_____

Depression

Psalm 42:5-6

_____
_____
_____

Proverbs 3:5-6

_____
_____
_____

Psalm 55:16-18

_____

_____

_____

Fear

Isaiah 42:10

_____

_____

_____

Psalm 23:4

_____

_____

_____

Psalm 34:4

_____

_____

_____

Guidance

James 1:5-6

_____

_____

_____

Psalm 25:9

_____

_____

_____

Psalm 32:8

_____
_____
_____

Guilt

Romans 8:1-2

_____
_____
_____

1John 1:9

_____
_____
_____

John 8:36

_____
_____
_____

Peace

John 14:27

_____
_____
_____

John 16:33

_____
_____
_____

Psalm 4:8

_____
_____
_____

Thankfulness

1Thessalonians 5:8

_____
_____
_____

Colossians 3:15

_____
_____
_____

Psalm 105:1

_____
_____
_____

Truth

John 14:1

_____
_____
_____

Psalm 37:3

_____
_____
_____

Psalm 40:4

_____

_____

_____

Wisdom

James 1:5-7

_____

_____

_____

Luke 21:5

_____

_____

_____

Proverbs 1:7

_____

_____

_____

Take the time to write out the previous scripture verses to help start the memorizing process as you feel led, and use the next few pages to write out some of your own:

_____

_____

_____

_____

_____

_____

_____

_____

_____

_____

_____

_____

_____

_____

_____

_____

_____

_____

_____

_____

_____

_____

_____

This section contains some of my own favorite memorization verses that may not have appeared so far in this book ...

Psalm 33:12

_____

_____

_____

Matthew 6:21

_____

_____

_____

Romans 10:17

_____

_____

_____

Matthew 18:20

_____

_____

_____

Matt 22:37

_____

_____

_____

Matthew 7:12

_____

_____

_____

1Timothy 4:8

_____

_____

_____

Romans 8:38-39

_____

_____

_____

Romans 12:12

_____

_____

_____

1Corinthians1:18

_____

_____

_____

Roman 8:18

_____
_____
_____

1Corinthians 15:33

_____
_____
_____

2Peter 1:3

_____
_____
_____

Isaiah 40:31

_____
_____
_____

John 14:6

_____
_____
_____

1Corinthians 2:9

_____
_____
_____

Psalm 37:4

_____
_____
_____

Proverbs 19:21

_____

_____

_____

ULTIMATE PRAYER JOURNAL

I'll start by giving you a few questions to answer and consider as topics for your Ultimate Prayer. A blank area follows where you can write your own topics to include in your Ultimate Prayer...

Whom should I pray for in my family?

_____

_____

_____

What specifically should I pray for them?

_____

_____

_____

_____

_____

Whom should I pray for in my life?

_____

_____

_____

What should I pray for them?

_____

_____

_____

_____

_____

What should I do with what you've given me financially?

_____

_____

_____

_____

_____

Where should I be spending my time?

_____

_____

_____

_____

_____

Are there areas in my life that should not be there?

_____

_____

_____

_____

_____

What is the Lord bringing on my heart right now about which to pray?

_____

_____

_____

_____

_____

Since praying more, what has started to change in my life?

_____

_____

_____

_____

_____

How have any of these prayers been answered?

_____

_____

_____

_____

_____

_____

_____

_____

_____

My own thankfulness, praises, questions, issues, struggles, weaknesses or battles to pray about or to pray for...

_____

_____

_____

_____

_____

_____

_____

_____

_____

_____

_____

_____

_____

_____

_____

_____

_____

_____

_____

_____

_____

_____

_____

_____

_____

I hope that these pages will motivate you to acquire a notebook and start your own prayer journal that becomes a testimony of the Lord in your life, for you to reflect on, and as a legacy for your family forever. May the Lord bless your efforts...

REFERENCES

Scripture:

The Holy Bible, New International Version. (2011). Grand Rapids, Michigan: Zondervan Publishing House. http://www.thenivbible.com/ (2016).

Definitions:

Acknowledge, Ask, Confess, Repent, Thanksgiving, Praise, Retreived from *www.dictionary.com, (2016).*

Songs:

Hall, Mark, (2003). *"Who am I,"* [Studio Album Casting Crowns, Recorded by Casting Crowns, Produced by Mark A. Miller and Steven Curtis Chapman; Nashville, Tennessee: Beach Street Records: Audio CD]. "Who Am I" received the awards for Song of the Year and Pop/Contemporary Recorded Song of the Year.

Chapman, Steven Curtis, (1994). *"Heaven in the Real World,"* [Heaven in the Real World, Recorded by Stephen Curtis Chapman, Produced by Phil Naish and Steven Curtis Chapman; Brentwood, Tennessee: Sparrow Records: Audio CD]. This song received the 1995 Gospel Music Association award for best Pop/Contemporary Song of the Year, and the album earned Pop/Contemporary Album of the Year.

US Religion Data:

Religious and Public Life, (2016), Pew Research Center. Retrieved from http://www.pewforum.org/religious-landscape-study/

World Lifespan Data:

Life Expectancy - Average Human Lifespan, (2015), *World Health Organization data.* Retrieved from Wikipedia.com, https://en.wikipedia.org/wiki/Life_expectancy

Printed in the United States
By Bookmasters